MW00860666

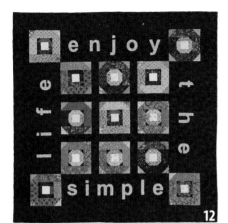

table of contents
scrap-lovers' quilts

2 make your point

8 broken dishes

12 enjoy the simple life

18 trail mix

24 square dance

30 living in the past

34 centennial pineapple

40 country charm

45 quilting basics

from the staff

Quilters of the past knew well the value of fabric scraps. Rather than discard outgrown clothes or excess fabric from a hand-sewn garment, quilters found that scraps were a thrifty way to turn something as small as a few fabric bits into a big beautiful quilt. Today's quilters still sew up scraps for many of the same reasons, but now doing so is more than just a necessity—it's a popular technique for quilters to create decorative items for their homes. With the added challenge to reduce stockpiles of scraps and to turn a hodgepodge of prints into something fantastic, quilters turn to scrap quilts as the perfect solution.

That's why we've created this book. Inside, you'll find an array of quilt designs using a variety of block motifs. From a contemporary wall hanging with an appliquéd message to a more traditional rotary-cut quilt using a myriad of prints, you're sure to find just the right project to put those scraps to good use.

have fun, scrap lovers!

1

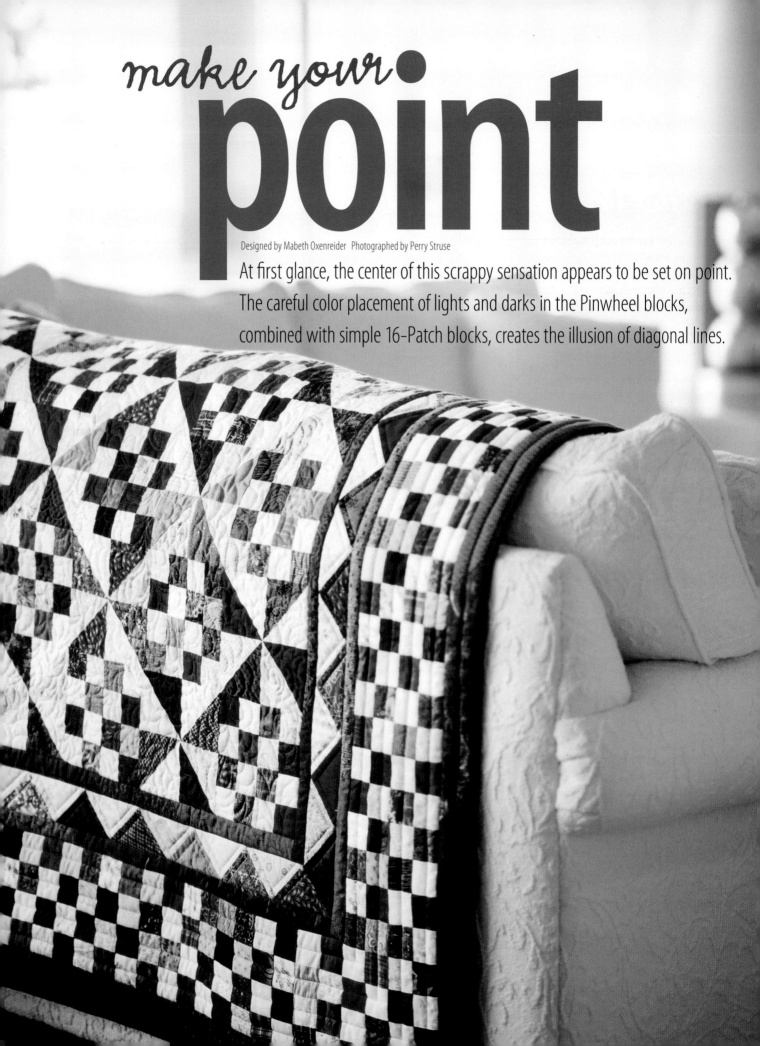

make your
point

Designed by Mabeth Oxenreider   Photographed by Perry Struse

At first glance, the center of this scrappy sensation appears to be set on point. The careful color placement of lights and darks in the Pinwheel blocks, combined with simple 16-Patch blocks, creates the illusion of diagonal lines.

materials

5¼ yards total of assorted dark prints for 16-Patch blocks, Pinwheel blocks, dogtooth border, and diagonally pieced borders

4¼ yards total of assorted light prints for 16-Patch blocks, Pinwheel blocks, and dogtooth border

¾ yard of red print for binding

5⅓ yards of backing fabric

84×96" of quilt batting

Finished quilt top: 77½×89½"
Finished 16-Patch block: 6" square
Finished Pinwheel block: 6" square

Quantities specified are for 44/45"-wide, 100% cotton fabrics. All measurements include a ¼" seam allowance. Sew with right sides together unless otherwise stated.

cut the fabrics

To make the best use of your fabrics, cut the pieces in the order that follows.

from assorted dark prints, cut:

- 38—2×42" strips
- Enough 2½"-wide strips in lengths varying from 8" to 22" to total 400" for diagonally pieced outer border
- Enough 1½"-wide strips in lengths varying from 8" to 22" to total 340" for diagonally pieced inner and middle borders
- Enough 1⅛"-wide strips in lengths varying from 8" to 22" to total 340" for diagonally pieced inner and middle borders
- 16—5½" squares, cutting each diagonally twice in an X for a total of 64 triangles (you'll have 2 triangles left over)
- 98—3⅞" squares

from assorted light prints, cut:

- 38—2×42" strips
- 15—5½" squares, cutting each diagonally twice in an X for a total of 60 triangles (you'll have 2 triangles left over)
- 98—3⅞" squares

from red print, cut:

- 9—2½×42" binding strips

assemble the 16-patch blocks

1. Aligning long edges and alternating dark and light, lay out two dark print 2×42" strips and two light print 2×42" strips; sew together to make a strip set (see Diagram 1). Press the seam allowances toward the dark print strips. Repeat with the remaining dark print and light print 2×42" strips to make a total of 19 strip sets. Cut the strip sets into 2"-wide segments for a total of 396. Set aside four segments for use in the outer border.

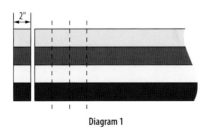

Diagram 1

2. Lay out four segments as shown in Diagram 2. Sew together the segments to make a 16-Patch block. Press the seam allowances in one direction. The 16-Patch block should measure 6½" square, including the seam allowances. Repeat to make a total of ninety-eight 16-Patch blocks.

Diagram 2

assemble the pinwheel blocks

1. Use a quilter's pencil to mark a diagonal line on the wrong side of the light print 3⅞" squares. (To prevent the fabric from stretching as you draw the lines, place 220-grit sandpaper under the squares.)

2. Layer a marked light print 3⅞" square atop each unmarked dark print 3⅞" square. Sew each pair together with two seams, stitching ¼" on each side of the drawn line (see Diagram 3).

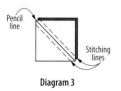

Diagram 3

To save time, chain-piece the layered squares. To chain-piece, machine-sew the pairs together one after the other without lifting the presser foot or clipping threads between pairs. First sew along one side of the drawn lines, then turn the group of pairs around and sew along the other side of the lines (see Diagram 4). Clip the connecting threads between pairs.

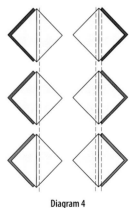

Diagram 4

3. Cut a pair apart on the drawn line to make two triangle units (see Diagram 5). Press the triangle units open to make two triangle-squares (see Diagram 6). Each triangle-square should measure 3½" square, including the seam allowances. Repeat to make a total of 196 triangle-squares.

Diagram 5

Diagram 6

4. Referring to Diagram 7 for placement, sew together four triangle-squares in pairs. Press the seam allowances in opposite directions. Then join the pairs to make a Pinwheel A block. Pieced Pinwheel A block should measure 6½" square, including the seam allowances. Repeat to make a total of 24 Pinwheel A blocks.

Diagram 7

5. Referring to Diagram 8, repeat Step 4 to make a total of 25 Pinwheel B blocks.

Diagram 8

assemble the quilt center

1. Referring to the Quilt Assembly Diagram on *page 6*, lay out 50 of the 16-Patch blocks alternately with the 49 Pinwheel blocks in 11 horizontal rows.

2. Sew together the blocks in each row. Press the seam allowances toward the Pinwheel blocks. Join the rows to make the quilt center. Press the seam allowances in one direction. The pieced quilt center should measure 54½×66½", including the seam allowances.

assemble and add the diagonally pieced inner border

1. Using diagonal seams, sew together assorted dark print 1½"-wide strips of varying lengths to make the following:

- 2—1½×54½" inner border strips

2. Using diagonal seams, sew together assorted dark print 1⅛"-wide strips of varying lengths to make the following:

- 2—1⅛×68½" inner border strips

3. Sew the short inner border strips to the short edges of the pieced quilt center. Then join the long inner border strips to the long edges of the pieced quilt center. Press all seam allowances toward the quilt center. The quilt center should now measure 55¾×68½", including the seam allowances.

assemble and add the dogtooth border

1. Referring to the Quilt Assembly Diagram, lay out 13 assorted light print triangles and 12 assorted dark print triangles in a row.

2. To assemble, layer two triangles with raw edges aligned, but ends offset by ¼" (see Diagram 9); sew together. Press the seam allowance toward the dark print fabric. Add the next triangle in the row to the pieced pair of triangles in the same manner (see Diagram 10).

Diagram 9

 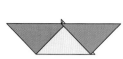

Diagram 10

Continue in this manner until all of the triangles in the row are sewn together to make a short dogtooth border strip.

3. Repeat steps 1 and 2 to make a second short dogtooth border strip.

4. Find the center point of a short dogtooth border strip and a short edge of the pieced quilt center; pin the border strip to the quilt center. Sew together. Press the seam allowance toward the inner border. Repeat with the remaining short dogtooth border strip and the opposite quilt center short edge.

5. In the same manner, lay out 16 assorted light print triangles alternately with 15 dark print triangles; sew together to make a long dogtooth border strip. Repeat to make a second long dogtooth border strip.

6. Find the center point of a long dogtooth border strip and a long edge of the pieced quilt center; pin the border strip to the quilt center. Sew together. Press the seam allowance toward the inner border. Repeat with the remaining long dogtooth border strip and the opposite quilt center long edge.

7. Pair the remaining eight dark print triangles; sew together to make border corners (see the Quilt Assembly Diagram). Press the seam allowances to one side. Join the border corners to the quilt center. Press the seam allowances toward the border corners. The pieced quilt center should now measure 60×72¾", including the seam allowances.

Quilt Assembly Diagram

assemble and add the diagonally pieced middle border

1. Using diagonal seams, sew together the remaining assorted dark print 1⅛"-wide strips of varying lengths to make the following:
- 2—1⅛×60" middle border strips

2. Using diagonal seams, sew together the remaining dark print 1½"-wide strips of varying lengths to make the following:
- 2—1½×74" middle border strips

3. Sew the short middle border strips to the short edges of the pieced quilt center. Then join the long middle border strips to the long edges of the pieced quilt center. Press all seam allowances toward the quilt center. The pieced quilt center should now measure 62×74", including the seam allowances.

assemble and add the 16-patch border

1. Referring to the Quilt Assembly Diagram *opposite,* lay out the remaining 16-Patch blocks in four rows of 12 blocks each. Sew together the blocks in each row to make four 16-Patch border strips. Press the seam allowances in one direction.

2. Add a remaining 2"-wide segment to one end of each 16-Patch border strip, paying attention to color placement (see the Quilt Assembly Diagram). Press the seam allowances in one direction.

3. Sew two 16-Patch border strips to the long edges of the pieced quilt center. Press the seam allowances toward the quilt center.

4. Sew the remaining 16-Patch border strips to the short edges of the quilt center. Press the seam allowances toward the quilt center. The quilt center should now measure 74×86", including the seam allowances.

assemble and add the diagonally pieced outer border

1. Using diagonal seams, sew together the dark print 2½" strips of varying lengths to make the following:
- 2—2½×90" outer border strips
- 2—2½×74" outer border strips

2. Sew the short outer border strips to the short edges of the pieced quilt center. Then join the long outer border strips to the long edges of the pieced quilt center to complete the quilt top. Press all seam allowances toward the quilt center.

complete the quilt

1. Layer the quilt top, batting, and backing according to the instructions in Quilting Basics, which begins on *page 45.*

2. Quilt as desired. Mabeth machine-quilted the center with an overall flowing feathered design. Quarter-inch outline quilting was used to enhance the dogtooth border, and a straight running stitch follows the rows of the 16-Patch border and diagonally pieced outer border.

3. Use the red print 2½×42" strips to bind the quilt according to the instructions in Quilting Basics.

color option

Vibrant colors draw the eye toward the triangle-squares in these Pinwheel blocks. Light prints for the 16-Patch blocks create little contrast, making them appear to recede.

broken dishes

Designed by Jill Kemp   Photographed by Perry Struse

Designer Jill Kemp's scrappy quilt showcases
a delightful assortment of favorite fabrics.

materials

9—⅛-yard pieces of assorted dark prints in red,
   green, brown, blue, and gold for blocks and border
⅝ yard of cream print for blocks
⅝ yard of green print for sashing and inner border
⅓ yard of gold plaid for pieced border

⅔ yard of dark gold print for outer border
⅓ yard of green plaid for binding
2⅛ yards of backing fabric
50" square of quilt batting

Finished quilt top: 44" square
Finished block: 8" square

Quantities specified for 44/45"-wide, 100% cotton
fabrics. All measurements include a ¼" seam
allowance. Sew with right sides together unless
otherwise indicated.

cut the fabrics

To make the best use of your fabrics, cut the
pieces in the order that follows.

from *each* of nine assorted dark prints, cut:
- 13—2⅞" squares, cutting each in half
  diagonally to make a total of 26 triangles

from cream print, cut:
- 80—2⅞" squares, cutting each in half
  diagonally to make a total of 160 triangles

from green print, cut:
- 6—2½×8½" sashing rectangles
- 4—2½×28½" sashing and inner
  border strips
- 2—2½×32½" inner border strips

from gold plaid, cut:
- 34—2⅞" squares, cutting each in half
  diagonally to make a total of 68 triangles

from dark gold print, cut:
- 4—4½×36½" outer border strips

from green plaid, cut:
- 5—2½×42" binding strips

assemble the broken dishes blocks

1. For one Broken Dishes block you'll need 16
triangles from one dark print and 16 cream
print triangles.

2. Sew together one dark print triangle and
one cream print triangle to make a triangle-
square (see Diagram 1). Press the seam
allowance toward the dark triangle. Repeat to
make a total of 16 triangle-squares.

Diagram 1

add the borders

1. Sew a green print 2½×28½" strip to opposite edges of the pieced quilt center. Then join a green print 2½×32½" inner border strip to the remaining edges of the quilt center. Press all seam allowances toward the green print inner border.

2. From the remaining assorted dark triangles, set aside four sets of four triangles each to use in the outer border.

3. Pair 68 of the remaining dark print triangles with the 68 gold plaid triangles; sew together in pairs to make 68 triangle-squares. (You should have six dark print triangles left over.) Press the seam allowances toward the dark print triangles.

4. Sew together 16 triangle-squares to make a short pieced border strip. Press the seam allowances in one direction. Repeat to make a second short pieced border strip. Sew the strips to opposite edges of the pieced quilt center. Press the seam allowances toward the green print inner border.

5. Sew together 18 triangle-squares to make a long pieced border strip. Press the seam allowances in one direction. Repeat to make a second long pieced border strip. Sew the strips to the remaining edges of the pieced quilt center. Press the seam allowances toward the green print inner border.

6. Pair each of the reserved four sets of dark print triangles with the remaining cream print triangles; sew together in pairs to make a total of 16 triangle-squares.

7. Referring to Diagram 3, *opposite,* sew together four matching triangle-squares in two rows. Press the seam allowances in opposite directions. Then join the rows to

3. Referring to Diagram 2 for placement, lay out the 16 triangle-squares in four horizontal rows. Sew together the triangle-squares in each row. Press the seam allowances in one direction, alternating the direction with each row. Then join the rows to make a Broken Dishes block. Press the seam allowances in one direction. The pieced Broken Dishes block should measure 8½" square, including seam allowances.

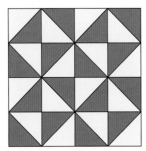

Diagram 2

4. Repeat steps 1 through 3 to make a total of nine Broken Dishes blocks.

assemble the quilt center

1. Referring to the photograph *above* for placement, lay out the nine pieced blocks, the six green print 2½×8½" sashing rectangles, and two green print 2½×28½" strips in vertical rows.

2. Sew together the blocks and sashing rectangles in each vertical row. Press the seam allowances toward the sashing rectangles. Then join the rows and green print 2½×28½" strips to make the quilt center. Press the seam allowances toward the sashing strips. The pieced quilt center should measure 28½" square, including the seam allowances.

make a border block. Press the seam allowance in one direction. The pieced border block should measure 4½" square, including the seam allowances. Repeat to make a total of four border blocks.

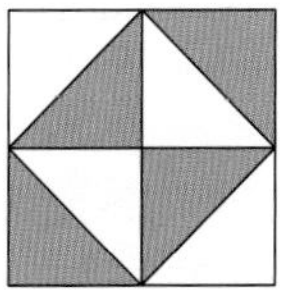

Diagram 3

8. Sew one dark gold print 4½×36½" outer border strip to opposite edges of the pieced quilt center. Press the seam allowances toward the dark gold print border.

9. Sew one border block to each end of the remaining dark gold print 4½×36½" outer border strips to make an outer border unit.

Press the seam allowances toward the dark gold print strip. Then join an outer border unit to the remaining edges of the pieced quilt center to complete the quilt top. Press the seam allowances toward the dark gold print outer border.

complete the quilt

1. Layer the quilt top, batting, and backing according to the instructions in Quilting Basics, which begins on *page 45*.

2. Quilt as desired. Jill hand-quilted in the ditch of each triangle-square. She added some additional straight lines of quilting in the outer border.

3. Use the green plaid 2½×42" strips to bind the quilt according to the instructions in Quilting Basics.

OPTIONAL SIZE CHART FOR BROKEN DISHES

ALTERNATE QUILT SIZES	TWIN	FULL/QUEEN	KING
No. of Blocks	35	56	81
No. of Blocks Wide by Long	5×7	7×8	9×9
Finished Size	64×84	84×94	104" square
YARDAGE REQUIREMENTS			
Total of assorted dark prints	2½ yards	3⅝ yards	4¾ yards
Total of cream print	2⅛ yards	3⅛ yards	4¼ yards
Total of green print	1⅛ yards	1½ yards	2½ yards
Total of gold plaid	⅝ yard	⅔ yard	¾ yard
Total of dark gold print	1 yard	1⅓ yards	1½ yards
Binding	⅝ yard	⅔ yard	⅞ yard
Backing	5 yards	7½ yards	9¼ yards
Batting	70×90"	90×100"	110" square

color option

The red and green prints in this three-block table runner version of "Broken Dishes" will add a bit of cheer to your dining room or kitchen table year-round.

Quilt tester Laura Boehnke used coordinating fabrics from her stash. Strong contrast between lights and darks in the pieced center blocks enhances the geometric pattern of the design.

enjoy the
simple life

Designed by Barbara Brandeburg
Photographed by Perry Struse and Marty Baldwin

Searching for a slow-down reminder? Gather your stash of country-style prints to piece the blocks for this comforting wall hanging or throw with an inspiring message. Because the project is quick and easy, you'll be snuggling under a new quilt in no time.

materials

- ⅛ yard total of assorted yellow prints for blocks
- ½ yard total of assorted red prints for blocks
- ½ yard total of assorted gold prints for blocks
- ⅜ yard total of assorted blue prints for blocks
- ⅜ yard total of assorted purple prints for blocks
- ½ yard total of assorted green prints for blocks and appliqués
- 3 yards of brown print for blocks, sashing, borders, and binding
- 3¼ yards of backing fabric
- 58" square of quilt batting
- Lightweight fusible web

Finished quilt top: 52" square
Finished block: 8" square

Quantities specified for 44/45"-wide, 100% cotton fabrics. All measurements include a ¼" seam allowance. Sew with right sides together unless otherwise stated.

cut the fabrics

To make the best use of your fabrics, cut the pieces in the order that follows. The letter patterns are on *page 17*. To use fusible web for appliquéing, as was done with this project, complete the following steps. **Note:** If you choose an alternate appliqué method other than fusible appliqué, the letter patterns will need to be reversed before making templates.

1. Lay the fusible web, paper side up, over the patterns. Use a pencil to trace each pattern the number of times indicated, leaving ½" between tracings. Cut out each piece roughly ¼" outside the traced lines.

2. Following the manufacturer's instructions, press the fusible-web shapes onto the back of the designated fabric; let cool. Cut out the fabric shapes on the drawn lines. Peel off the paper backings.

from assorted yellow prints, cut:
- 13—2½" squares for position 1

from assorted red prints, cut:
- 8—2½×8½" rectangles for positions 8 and 9
- 8—2½×4½" rectangles for positions 6 and 7
- 12—1½×4½" rectangles for positions 4 and 5
- 12—1½×2½" rectangles for positions 2 and 3

from assorted gold prints, cut:
- 6—2½×8½" rectangles for positions 8 and 9
- 6—2½×4½" rectangles for positions 6 and 7
- 14—1½×4½" rectangles for positions 4 and 5
- 14—1½×2½" rectangles for positions 2 and 3

from assorted blue prints, cut:
- 6—2½×8½" rectangles for positions 8 and 9
- 6—2½×4½" rectangles for positions 6 and 7

from assorted purple prints, cut:
- 6—2½×8½" rectangles for positions 8 and 9
- 6—2½×4½" rectangles for positions 6 and 7

from assorted green prints, cut:
- 52—2½" squares
- 4 *each* of the letter E
- 2 *each* of the letters I and L
- 1 *each* of the letters F, J, H, M, N, O, P, S, T, and Y

from brown print, cut:
- 6—4½×42" strips for outer border
- 6—2½×42" binding strips
- 4—8½×28½" inner border strips
- 2—2½×28½" sashing strips
- 6—2½×8½" sashing strips
- 52—1½" squares

designer notes

To ensure proper placement when Barbara Brandeburg appliquéd the letters to the inner border, she first sewed the inner border strips to the quilt center using long basting stitches; then she fused the letters in place. After fusing, Barbara removed the inner border so that she would have less fabric to work with as she machine-appliquéd. With large letters such as these, she used a slightly longer than usual machine blanket stitch to hold the letters securely. After appliquéing the letters, she resewed the border to the quilt center.

assemble the blocks

1. Sew red position 2 and 3 rectangles to opposite edges of a yellow print position 1 square to make a center subunit (see Diagram 1). Press the seam allowances toward the red print rectangles. The pieced center subunit should measure 2½×4½", including the seam allowances.

Diagram 1

2. Referring to Diagram 2, add red print positions 4 and 5 rectangles to the long edges of the center subunit to make a center square unit. Press the seam allowances toward the red print rectangles.

Diagram 2

3. For accurate sewing lines, use a quilter's pencil to mark a diagonal line on the wrong side of four brown print 1½" squares. (To prevent the fabric from stretching as you draw the lines, place 220-grit sandpaper under the squares.)

4. Align a marked brown print 1½" square atop each corner of the center square unit (see Diagram 3, noting the direction of the marked lines). Stitch on the marked lines; trim away the excess fabric, leaving ¼" seam allowances. Press the attached triangles open to make a red-center square.

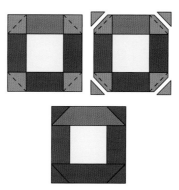

Diagram 3

5. Add assorted gold print positions 6, 7, 8, and 9 rectangles in pairs according to the numerical sequence indicated on Diagram 4. Press all seam allowances toward the red-center square.

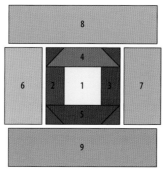

Diagram 4

6. Referring to steps 3 and 4, mark four assorted green print 2½" squares. Stitch them to the Step 5 square as before; trim and press to make a red-center block (see Diagram 5). The pieced red-center block should measure 8½" square, including the seam allowances.

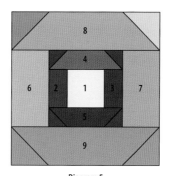

Diagram 5

7. Repeat steps 1 through 6 to make a total of six red-center blocks as follows: three blocks with assorted gold prints in positions 6–9, two with assorted blue prints in positions 6–9, and one with assorted purple prints in positions 6–9.

8. Repeat steps 1 through 4 using assorted gold prints in positions 2–5 to make a gold-center square (see Diagram 6). Repeat to make a total of seven gold-center squares.

Diagram 6

9. Repeat steps 5 and 6 to make a total of seven gold-center blocks as follows: four blocks with assorted red prints in positions 6–9, two blocks with assorted purple prints in positions 6–9, and one block with assorted blue prints in positions 6–9.

assemble the quilt center

1. Referring to the Quilt Assembly Diagram, lay out three red-center blocks, six gold-center blocks, six 2½×8½" sashing strips, and two 2½×28½" sashing strips in five horizontal rows.

2. Sew together the pieces in each row. Press the seam allowances toward the sashing strips. Then join the rows to make the quilt center. Press the seam allowances in one direction. The pieced quilt center should measure 28½" square, including the seam allowances.

Quilt Assembly Diagram

add and appliqué the inner border

1. Sew brown print 8½×28½" inner border strips to opposite edges of the pieced quilt center. Press the seam allowances toward the border.

2. Referring to the Quilt Assembly Diagram, sew the remaining red-center and gold-center blocks to each end of the remaining brown print 8½×28½" inner border strips to make two pieced border strips. Press the seam allowances toward the brown print strips. Sew the pieced border strips to the remaining edges of the pieced quilt center. Press the seam allowances toward the border. The pieced quilt center should now measure 44½" square, including the seam allowances.

3. Position the green print letters on the quilt top; fuse in place. Machine-blanket-stitch around the letters. *Note:* Designer Barbara Brandeburg used a thread color that matched the green print she used for the letters to minimize contrast between the fabric and thread. If your prefer a more folk art appearance, use black thread for the machine blanket stitching. Or use perle cotton or embroidery floss to blanket-stitch around the letters by hand.

add the outer border

1. Cut and piece the brown print 4½×42" strips to make the following:
- 2—4½×52½" outer border strips
- 2—4½×44½" outer border strips

2. Sew the short outer border strips to opposite edges of the pieced quilt center. Sew the long outer border strips to the remaining edges of the quilt center to complete the quilt top. Press all seam allowances toward the border.

complete the quilt

1. Layer the quilt top, batting, and backing according to the instructions in Quilting Basics, which begins on *page 45*.

2. Quilt as desired. Barbara machine-stitched all the blocks in the ditch and stipple-quilted the borders and sashing.

3. Use the brown print 2½×42" strips to bind the quilt according to the instructions in Quilting Basics.

enjoy this flip

color option

If your idea of the simple life could stand a little jazzing up, then this contemporary color option might just fit the bill. Black-and-white "optical illusion" prints for the block centers and the sashing mingle with splashes of vibrant retro colors in the remainder of the quilt. A novelty print for the border is a wholecloth design that looks pieced but isn't—it makes the finished quilt look more complex than it really is.

trail mix

If you have a big stash of fabric scraps, designer Mabeth Oxenreider has the perfect project for you to put them to good use.

Designed by Mabeth Oxenreider   Photographed by Perry Struse

materials

7½ yards total of assorted light, medium, and dark prints for blocks (see Designer Notes on page 21)
½ yard of purple print for inner border
⅔ yard of gold print for middle border and piping
2 yards of green print for outer border and binding
7½ yards of backing fabric
90×108" of quilt batting

Finished quilt top: 83½×101½"
Finished blocks: 6" square

Quantities specified for 44/45"-wide, 100% cotton fabrics. All measurements include a ¼" seam allowance. Sew with right sides together unless otherwise stated.

cut the fabrics

To make the best use of your fabrics, cut the border, piping, and binding pieces in the order that follows. Because of the variety of fabrics used to make this quilt, cutting instructions for individual blocks follow in each section.

from purple print, cut:
- 9—1½×42" strips for inner border

from gold print, cut:
- 9—1¼×42" strips for middle border
- 10—¾×42" strips for piping

from green print, cut:
- 9—4½×42" strips for outer border
- 10—2½×42" binding strips

cut and assemble the four-patch blocks

1. To make one Four-Patch block, cut the following:

from assorted prints, cut:
- 4—3½" squares

2. Sew together the squares in pairs (see Diagram 1). Press the seam allowances in opposite directions. Sew together the pairs to make a Four-Patch block. Press the seam allowance in one direction. The Four-Patch block should measure 6½" square, including the seam allowances.

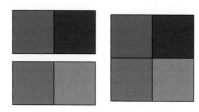

Diagram 1

3. Repeat steps 1 and 2 to make a total of 32 Four-Patch blocks.

cut and assemble the double four-patch blocks

1. To make one Double Four-Patch block, cut the following:

from assorted prints, cut:
- 2—3½" squares
- 8—2" squares

2. Sew together four 2" squares in pairs (see Diagram 2). Press the seam allowances in opposite directions. Sew together the pairs to make a Four-Patch unit. Press the seam allowance in one direction. The Four-Patch unit should measure 3½" square, including the seam allowances. Repeat to make a second Four-Patch unit.

Diagram 2

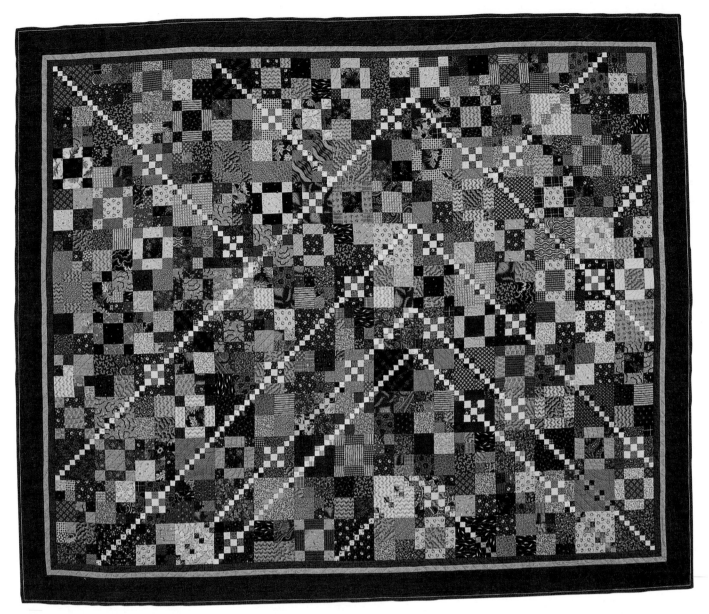

3. Sew together two 3½" squares and the two Four-Patch units in pairs (see Diagram 3). Press the seam allowances toward the 3½" squares. Join the pairs to make a Double Four-Patch block. Press the seam allowance in one direction. The pieced Double Four-Patch block should measure 6½" square, including the seam allowances.

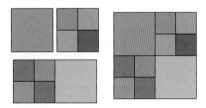

Diagram 3

4. Repeat steps 1 through 3 to make a total of 38 Double Four-Patch blocks.

cut and assemble the triple four-patch blocks

1. To make one Triple Four-Patch block, cut the following:

from one assorted print, cut:

- 2—3½" squares
- 4—2" squares

from a medium or dark print, cut:

- 1—1¼×12" strip

from a light print, cut:

- 1—1¼×12" strip

2. Aligning long edges, sew together the medium or dark print 1¼×12" strip and the light print 1¼×12" strip to make a strip set (see Diagram 4). Press the seam allowance toward the darker strip. Cut the strip set into eight 1¼"-wide segments.

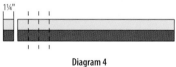

Diagram 4

3. Sew together two Step 2 segments as shown in Diagram 5 to make a Four-Patch unit. The pieced Four-Patch unit should measure 2" square, including the seam allowances. Repeat to make a total of four Four-Patch units.

Diagram 5

Note: To speed up the cutting and piecing of the Four-Patch units, Mabeth suggests using the strip-piecing technique. After assembling a strip set, cut it in half. Layer the two halves with right sides together, making sure the light strip from one half is atop the dark strip from the other half (see Diagram 6). Because the seam allowances are pressed toward the dark strip, they're now in opposite directions, causing the two halves to "lock" in place. Cut the layered strip set into 1¼"-wide segments; then sew the layered segments together along one edge to make Four-Patch units. Carefully handle the segments as you move them to the sewing machine so you don't "unlock" the seams.

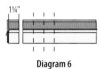

Diagram 6

4. Sew together two Four-Patch units and two 2" squares in pairs (see Diagram 7, noting the placement of the light squares in the Four-Patch units). Press the seam allowances toward the 2" squares. Join the pairs to make a Double Four-Patch unit. Press the seam allowance in one direction. The pieced Double Four-Patch unit should measure 3½" square, including the seam allowances. Repeat to make a second Double Four-Patch unit.

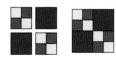

Diagram 7

5. Sew together the two Double Four-Patch units and the two 3½" squares in pairs (see Diagram 8). Press the seam allowances toward the 3½" squares. Join the pairs to make a Triple Four-Patch block. Press the seam allowance in one direction. The Triple Four-Patch block should measure 6½" square, including the seam allowances.

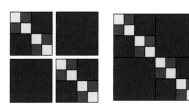

Diagram 8

6. Repeat steps 1 through 5 to make a total of 44 Triple Four-Patch blocks.

cut and assemble the double nine-patch blocks

1. To make one Double Nine-Patch block, cut the following:

from assorted prints, cut:
- 2—2" squares

from one assorted print, cut:
- 4—2×3½" rectangles

from a medium or dark print, cut:
- 4—1½" squares
- 4—1¼" squares

from a light print, cut:
- 5—1½" squares
- 4—1¼" squares

2. Sew together two medium or dark print 1¼" squares and two light print 1¼" squares in pairs. Press the seam allowances in opposite directions. Sew together the pairs to make a Four-Patch unit (see Diagram 9). Press the seam allowance in one direction. The pieced Four-Patch unit should measure 2" square, including the seam allowances. Repeat to make a second Four-Patch unit.

Diagram 9

3. Referring to Diagram 10, lay out four medium or dark print 1½" squares and five light print 1½" squares in three rows. Sew together the squares in rows. Press the seam allowances toward the darker squares. Then join the rows to make a Nine-Patch unit. Press the seam allowances in one direction. The pieced Nine-Patch unit should measure 3½" square, including the seam allowances.

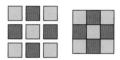

Diagram 10

4. Referring to Diagram 11, lay out the two 2" squares, the two Four-Patch units, the one Nine-Patch unit, and the four 2×3½" rectangles in three rows. Sew together the pieces in rows. Press the seam allowances toward the rectangles. Then join the rows to make a Double Nine-Patch block. Press the seam allowances in one direction. The pieced block should measure 6½" square, including the seam allowances.

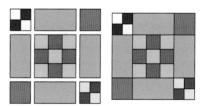

Diagram 11

designer notes

While the piecing of this quilt top is relatively simple, gathering a variety of fabric scraps, such as designer Mabeth Oxenreider used to make the photographed quilt, could take a while. That's why the yardage requirement for the blocks is specified as a total amount (see Materials on page 18) rather than being identified by fabric color.

Mabeth chose prints with lots of texture, value, and scale, and used light shirtings in the Triple Four-Patch blocks. She also found that reproduction fabrics work well. She suggests avoiding tone-on-tone prints, as they appear solid from a distance.

Mabeth pieced 180 blocks in five different patterns to compose this quilt. If you want to make a less scrappy version, strip piecing may simplify the construction.

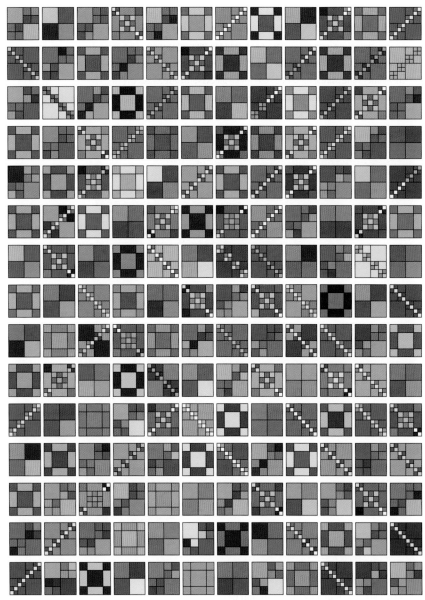

Quilt Assembly Diagram

5. Repeat steps 1 through 4 to make a total of 24 Double Nine-Patch blocks.

cut and assemble the nine-patch blocks

1. To make one Nine-Patch block, cut the following:

from one assorted print, cut:
- 1—3½" square
- 4—2" squares

from a second assorted print, cut:
- 4—2×3½" rectangles

2. Referring to Diagram 12, lay out the four 2" squares, the 3½" square, and the four 2×3½" rectangles. Sew together the pieces in rows. Press the seam allowances toward the darker pieces. Then join the rows to make a Nine-Patch block. Press the seam allowances in one direction. The pieced block should measure 6½" square, including the seam allowances.

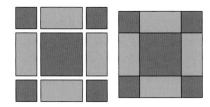

Diagram 12

3. Repeat steps 1 and 2 to make a total of 42 Nine-Patch blocks.

assemble the quilt center

1. Referring to the Quilt Assembly Diagram, lay out the 32 Four-Patch blocks, the 38 Double Four-Patch blocks, the 44 Triple Four-Patch blocks, the 24 Double Nine-Patch blocks, and the 42 Nine-Patch blocks in 15 horizontal rows.

2. Sew together the blocks in each row. Press the seam allowances in one direction, alternating directions with each row. Then join the rows to make the quilt center; press. The pieced quilt center should measure 72½×90½", including the seam allowances.

add the borders

1. Cut and piece the purple print 1½×42" strips to make the following:
- 2—1½×92½" inner border strips
- 2—1½×72½" inner border strips

2. Sew the short purple print inner border strips to the top and bottom edges of the pieced quilt center. Then join the long purple print inner border strips to the side edges of the quilt center. Press all seam allowances toward the purple print border.

3. Cut and piece the gold print 1¼×42" strips to make the following:
- 2—1¼×94" middle border strips
- 2—1¼×74½" middle border strips

4. Sew the short gold print middle border strips to the top and bottom edges of the pieced quilt center. Then join the long gold print middle border strips to the side edges of the quilt center. Press all seam allowances toward the gold print border.

5. Cut and piece the green print 4½×42" strips to make the following:
- 2—4½×102" outer border strips
- 2—4½×76" outer border strips

6. Sew the short green print outer border strips to the top and bottom edges of the pieced quilt center. Then join the long green print outer border strips to the side edges of the quilt center to complete the quilt top. Press all seam allowances toward the green print border.

complete the quilt

1. Layer the quilt top, batting, and backing according to the instructions in Quilting Basics, which begins on *page 45*.

2. Quilt as desired. Mabeth machine-quilted parallel lines, cables, and swirls on her quilt top, diagonally orienting her stitches along the same lines as the Triple Four-Patch blocks. She extended her designs onto the borders.

color option

By experimenting with block placement, Trail Mix will amaze you with the abundance of design options to explore. In this version made with Americana prints, the Triple Four-Patch blocks form a secondary diamond pattern in the quilt center. Even though piping was eliminated, the original triple border combination remains to give this 9×9 block version additional depth.

3. Cut and piece the gold print ¾×42" strips to make the following:
- 1—¾×385" piping strip

4. With wrong side inside, fold and press the gold print strip in half lengthwise to make ⅜"-wide piping.

5. Aligning raw edges and using a ¼" seam, baste the piping strip to the quilt top; miter the corners. (For information on mitering, see Quilting Basics.)

6. Use the green print 2½×42" strips to bind the quilt according to the instructions in Quilting Basics. *Note:* About ⅛" of the gold piping will show between the quilt top and binding edge once the binding is turned back.

square dance

Designed by Jackie Conaway   Photographed by Perry Struse

Simple squares and triangles join to make designer Jackie Conaway's table topper. The secondary diamond pattern emerges with a change in the orientation of the blocks' seams.

materials

- 1½ yards total of assorted light prints for blocks and pieced border
- 1⅓ yards total of assorted dark prints for blocks and pieced border
- ½ yard of tan print for inner border
- 1 yard of brown print for outer border and binding

- 2½ yards of backing fabric
- 44×56" of quilt batting

- Finished quilt top: 38×50"
- Finished block: 6" square

Quantities specified for 44/45"-wide, 100% cotton fabrics. All measurements include a ¼" seam allowance. Sew with right sides together unless otherwise stated.

select the fabrics

Designer Jackie Conaway used 21 light prints and 21 dark prints to achieve the desired scrappiness of her quilt. Use the total yardage as a guideline when selecting fabrics from your stash.

cut the fabrics

To make the best use of your fabrics, cut the pieces in the order that follows.

from assorted light prints, cut:
- 118—2⅞" squares
- 52—2½" squares
- 8—2⅜" squares

from assorted dark prints, cut:
- 118—2⅞" squares
- 8—2⅜" squares

from tan print, cut:
- 2—2½×36½" inner border strips
- 2—2½×28½" inner border strips

from brown print, cut:
- 4—3½×42" strips for outer border
- 5—2½×42" binding strips

make the triangle-squares

1. Use a quilter's pencil to mark a diagonal line on the wrong side of the assorted light print 2⅞" squares. (To prevent the fabric from stretching as you draw the lines, place 220-grit sandpaper under the squares.)

2. Layer each marked light print square atop an unmarked dark print 2⅞" square. Sew each pair together with two seams, stitching ¼" on each side of the drawn line (see Diagram 1).

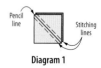

Diagram 1

To save time, chain-piece the layered squares. To chain-piece, machine-sew the pairs together one after the other without lifting the presser foot or clipping threads between units. First sew along one side of the drawn lines, then turn the group of pairs around and sew along the other side of the lines (see Diagram 2). Clip the connecting threads between pairs.

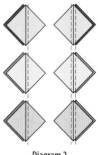

Diagram 2

3. Cut a pair apart on the drawn line to make two triangle units (see Diagram 3). Press the triangle units open to make two large triangle-squares (see Diagram 4). Each large triangle-square should measure 2½" square, including the seam allowances.

Diagram 3

Diagram 4

4. Repeat Step 3 to make a total of 236 large triangle-squares.

5. Repeat steps 1 through 3 using the eight light print 2⅜" squares and the eight dark print 2⅜" squares to make a total of 16 small triangle-squares. Set them aside for the outer border.

assemble the blocks

1. Referring to Diagram 5 for placement, lay out seven large triangle-squares and two assorted light print 2½" squares in three horizontal rows, noting the direction of the triangle-squares' seams.

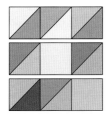

Diagram 5

2. Sew together the pieces in each row. Press the seam allowances in one direction, alternating the direction with each row. Then join the rows to make a block. Press the seam allowances toward the squares. The pieced block should measure 6½" square, including the seam allowances.

3. Repeat steps 1 and 2 to make a total of 24 blocks.

assemble the quilt center

1. Referring to the Quilt Assembly Diagram, lay out the 24 blocks in six horizontal rows, noting the direction of the triangle-squares' seams in each block. Rotating the blocks makes the diamond pattern emerge in the completed quilt center.

2. Sew together the blocks in each row. Press the seam allowances in one direction, alternating the direction with each row. Then join the rows to complete the quilt center. Press the seam allowances in one direction. The pieced quilt center should measure 24½×36½", including the seam allowances.

Quilt Assembly Diagram

designer notes

Jackie Conaway and her daughter, Terri Degenkolb, design quilt patterns for their company, Whimsicals. Mother and daughter each have different loves when it comes to designing.

"Mom is more traditional in her piecing," Terri says, "and I like to doodle. But, for most of our designs, we love to combine them for a whimsical look."

"This design was originally done to use up a stash of Christmas fabrics that had been waiting for a project," Jackie says. "The block started out to be all triangle-squares, but that proved to be too much of a good thing, and the overall design was boring. Adding the two solid squares gave just a bit of interest to the square that appears when four blocks are rotated and stitched together."

add the borders

1. Add the tan print 2½×36½" inner border strips to the side edges of the pieced quilt center. Then join the tan print 2½×28½" inner border strips to the top and bottom edges of the pieced quilt center. Press all seam allowances toward the inner border.

2. Sew together 20 large triangle-squares to make a side pieced border unit. Note the direction of the triangle-square seams in the photograph on *page 26*. Press the seam allowances in one direction. The side pieced border unit should measure 2½×40½", including the seam allowances. Repeat to make a second side pieced border unit. Sew the units to the side edges of the pieced quilt center. Press the seam allowances toward the inner border.

3. Sew together 14 large triangle-squares to make a top pieced border unit. Note the direction of the triangle-square seams in the photograph on *page 26*. Press the seam allowances in one direction. The top pieced border unit should measure 2½×28½", including the seam allowances. Add a light print 2½" square to each end of the top pieced border unit. Press the seam allowances toward the light print squares. Repeat to make a bottom pieced border unit. Add the top and bottom pieced border units to the remaining edges of the pieced quilt center. Press the seam allowances toward the inner border.

4. Cut and piece the brown print 3½×42" strips to make the following:
- 2—3½×44½" outer border strips
- 2—3½×32½" outer border strips

OPTIONAL SIZE CHART FOR SQUARE DANCE			
ALTERNATE QUILT SIZES	TWIN	FULL/QUEEN	KING
No. of Blocks	96	168	256
No. of Blocks Wide by Long	8×12	12×14	16×16
Finished Size	62×86"	86×98"	110" square
YARDAGE REQUIREMENTS			
Total of assorted light prints	3⅞ yards	6 yards	8⅝ yards
Total of assorted dark prints	3 yards	4½ yards	6⅓ yards
Tan print	¾ yard	⅞ yard	1 yard
Brown print	1¾ yards	2 yards	2⅜ yards
Backing	5⅛ yards	7⅔ yards	9⅔ yards
Batting	68×92"	92×104"	116" square

5. Add the long brown print outer border strips to the side edges of the pieced quilt center. Press the seam allowances toward the outer border.

6. Sew together four small triangle-squares in pairs (see Diagram 6). Press the seam allowances in opposite directions. Then join the pairs to make a border corner block. Press the seam allowance in one direction. The border corner block should measure 3½" square, including the seam allowances. Repeat to make a total of four border corner blocks.

Diagram 6

7. Sew a border corner block to each end of the short brown print outer border strips. Press the seam allowances toward the brown print strips. Join the pieced outer border strips to the top and bottom edges of the pieced quilt center to complete the quilt top. Press the seam allowances toward the outer border.

complete the quilt

1. Layer the quilt top, batting, and backing according to the instructions in Quilting Basics, which begins on *page 45*. Quilt as desired.

2. Use the brown print 2½×42" strips to bind the quilt according to the instructions in Quilting Basics.

color option

For this 16-block wall hanging, quilt tester Laura Boehnke used an assortment of bright batiks. "I reversed the placement of the lights and darks in my quilt," Laura says. "My lights were yellows, oranges, and pinks, and my darks were blues and purples.

"I was deliberate in placing the lights so that the yellow prints formed the larger squares around the pink center square. Using oranges and a few pinks for the light triangles that finish off the quilt center makes them recede, adding more pop to the yellows."

living in the
past

Designed by Alice Berg   Photographed by Perry Struse

A circa-1885 Pennsylvania quilt inspired this antique-looking coverlet.

materials

3 yards total of assorted light and dark prints for Ohio Star blocks (see Designer Notes on page 33)

3—⅓-yard pieces of assorted brown prints for setting squares

1¼ yards of brown star print for setting squares, setting triangles, and corner triangles

2 yards of gold print for border and binding

4⅛ yards of backing fabric

74" square of quilt batting

Finished quilt top: 69" square
Finished Ohio Star block: 10" square

Quantities specified for 44/45"-wide, 100% cotton fabrics. All measurements include a ¼" seam allowance unless otherwise stated.

from brown star print, cut:
- 3—10½" squares for setting squares
- 3—15½" squares, cutting each diagonally twice in an X for a total of 12 setting triangles
- 2—8" squares, cutting each in half diagonally for a total of 4 corner triangles

from gold print, cut:
- 2—6½×57½" border strips
- 2—6½×69½" border strips
- 7—2½×42" binding strips

cut the fabrics

To make the best use of your fabrics, cut the pieces in the order that follows. There are no pattern pieces; the letter designations are for placement only.

For this project, the border strips are cut lengthwise (parallel to the selvage). You may wish to add extra length to the strips when cutting them to allow for possible sewing differences.

from assorted light and dark prints, cut the following for *each* of 16 ohio star blocks:
- 1—3" square for position A
- 4—1¾×3" rectangles for position B
- 8—1¾" squares for position C
- 4—1¾" squares for position D
- 4—3×5½" rectangles for position E
- 8—3" squares for position F
- 4—3" squares for position G

from *each* of three assorted brown prints, cut:
- 2—10½" squares for setting squares

assemble the ohio star blocks

The following instructions are for making one Ohio Star block. Repeat the steps to make a total of 16 blocks.

1. For accurate sewing lines, use a quilter's pencil to mark a diagonal line on the wrong side of the eight C squares and the eight F squares. (To prevent your fabric from stretching as you draw the lines, place 220-grit sandpaper under the squares.)

2. With right sides together, align a marked C square with one end of a B rectangle (see Diagram 1; note the placement of the marked diagonal line). Stitch on the marked line; trim away the excess fabric, leaving a ¼" seam allowance. Press the attached triangle open.

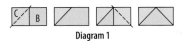
Diagram 1

3. In the same manner, align a second marked C square with the opposite end of the B rectangle (see Diagram 1, again noting the placement of the marked diagonal line). Stitch on the marked line; trim and press as before to make a small Flying Geese unit. The pieced small Flying Geese unit should still measure 1¾×3", including the seam allowances.

4. Repeat steps 2 and 3 to make a total of four small Flying Geese units.

5. Referring to Diagram 2 for placement, lay out the four small Flying Geese units, one A square, and the four D squares in three horizontal rows. Sew together the pieces in each row. Press the seam allowances toward the squares. Then join the rows to make an Ohio Star unit. Press the seam allowances in one direction. The pieced Ohio Star unit should measure 5½" square, including the seam allowances.

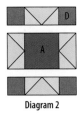
Diagram 2

6. Repeat steps 2 and 3 using the E rectangles and F squares to make a total of four large Flying Geese units. The pieced large Flying Geese units should measure 3×5½", including the seam allowances.

7. Referring to Diagram 3 for placement, lay out the pieced Ohio Star unit, the four large Flying Geese units, and the four G squares in three horizontal rows. Sew together the pieces in each row. Press the seam allowances toward the G squares or Ohio Star unit. Then join the rows to make an Ohio Star block. Press the seam allowances in one direction. The pieced Ohio Star block should measure 10½" square, including the seam allowances.

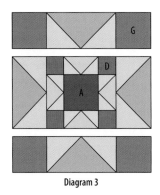
Diagram 3

assemble the quilt center

1. Referring to the photograph on *page 33* for placement, lay out the 16 Ohio Star blocks, the assorted brown print 10½" setting squares, and the brown star print setting triangles in diagonal rows. Sew together the pieces in each row. Press the seam allowances toward the setting squares and triangles.

2. Join the diagonal rows. Press the seam allowances in one direction. Add the brown star print corner triangles to complete the quilt center. The pieced quilt center should measure 57½" square, including the seam allowances.

add the border

Sew a gold print 6½×57½" border strip to the top and bottom edges of the pieced quilt center. Then add a gold print 6½×69½" border strip to each side edge of the pieced quilt center to complete the quilt top. Press all seam allowances toward the gold print border.

complete the quilt

1. Layer the quilt top, batting, and backing according to the instructions in Quilting Basics, which begins on *page 45*. Quilt as desired. Alice hand-quilted a feather design in each of the setting squares and triangles. She hand-quilted a 1½"-wide crosshatch in the border.

2. Use the gold print 2½×42" strips to bind the quilt according to the instructions in Quilting Basics.

color options

For a traditional look, this red, yellow, and blue Country French version *top right* would make a welcome addition to a kitchen or dining area.

Vibrant Ohio Star blocks radiate against a stunning rainforest-theme background on the quilt *bottom right*. In the middle of each block, a different animal was fussy-cut and pieced in the center square.

designer notes

Because "Living in the Past" is a scrappy quilt, designer Alice Berg suggests incorporating small amounts of numerous fabrics. For instance, she recommends using a large selection of fat quarters and several ½-yard pieces, repeating the fabrics throughout the quilt.

centennial pineapple

The Pineapple block, a variation of the Log Cabin, shows a quilter's interpretation of the jagged edges of the tropical fruit.

Designed by Judy Martin
Photographed by Hopkins Associates

materials

1⅔ yards total of assorted cream prints for blocks
2½ yards total of assorted prints in red, blue, navy, gold, pink, olive, and brown for blocks
½ yard of blue print for binding
2⅞ yards of backing fabric
50" square of quilt batting

Finished quilt top: 44" square
Finished block: 11" square

Quantities specified for 44/45"-wide, 100% cotton fabrics. All measurements include a ¼" seam allowance. Sew with right sides together unless otherwise stated.

cut the fabrics

To make the best use of your fabrics, cut the pieces in the order that follows. The patterns begin on *page 38*. To make templates of the patterns, follow the instructions in Quilting Basics, which begins on *page 45*.

from assorted cream prints, cut:
- 64 *each* of patterns A, C, E, G, and I

from assorted red, blue, navy, gold, pink, olive, and brown prints, cut:
- 64 *each* of patterns B, D, F, H, J, and K

from blue print, cut:
- 5—2×42" binding strips

assemble the pinwheel units

1. Referring to Diagram 1 for placement, sew together a cream print A triangle and a dark print B piece to make an AB unit. Press the seam allowance toward the dark print piece. Repeat to make a total of 64 AB units.

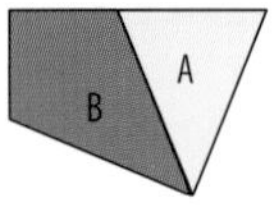

Diagram 1

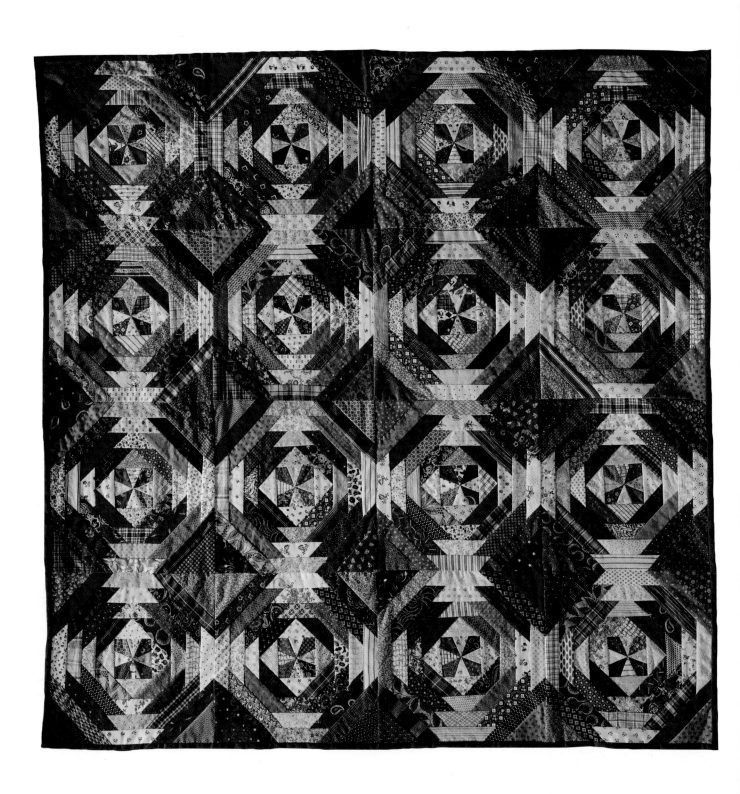

2. Sew together two AB units to make a pinwheel half (see Diagram 2). Press the seam allowance toward the light print piece. Repeat to make a total of 32 pinwheel halves.

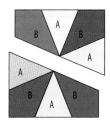

Diagram 2

3. Join two pinwheel halves to make a pinwheel unit (see Diagram 3). Press the seam allowance open. Each pinwheel unit should measure 3" square, including seam allowances. Repeat to make a total of 16 pinwheel units.

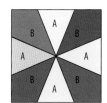

Diagram 3

assemble the blocks

1. Sew cream print C triangles to opposite edges of a pinwheel unit (see Diagram 4). Press the seam allowances toward the triangles. Sew cream print C triangles to the remaining edges of the pinwheel unit to make a block center. Press the seam allowances toward the triangles.

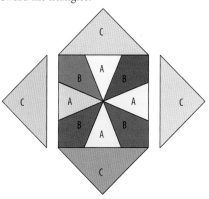

Diagram 4

2. Referring to the Block Assembly Diagram and working in alphabetical order, sew four of each remaining piece to the block center, joining them in pairs to opposite edges as in Step 1, to make a Pineapple block. Press the seam allowances away from the block center; use a pressing cloth to avoid developing a fabric "shine." The pieced Pineapple block should measure 11½" square, including the seam allowances.

Block Assembly Diagram

3. Repeat steps 1 and 2 to make a total of 16 Pineapple blocks.

color option

If you're wanting a less scrappy and more controlled look for your quilt, try using one dark and one light to make a striking rendition of Centennial Pineapple. The placement of the contrasting fabric emphasizes the pointed edges of the pieces in this quilt.

assemble the quilt top

1. Referring to the photograph *opposite*, lay out the Pineapple blocks in four horizontal rows.

2. Sew together the blocks in one row. Press the seam allowances in one direction, alternating the direction with each row. Then join the rows to complete the quilt top. Press the seam allowances in one direction.

complete the quilt

1. Layer the quilt top, batting, and backing according to the instructions in Quilting Basics, which begins on *page 45*. Quilt as desired.

2. Use the blue print 2×42" strips to bind the quilt according to the instructions in Quilting Basics.

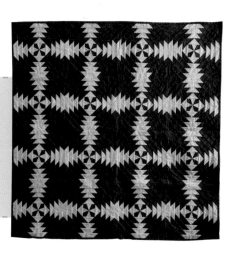

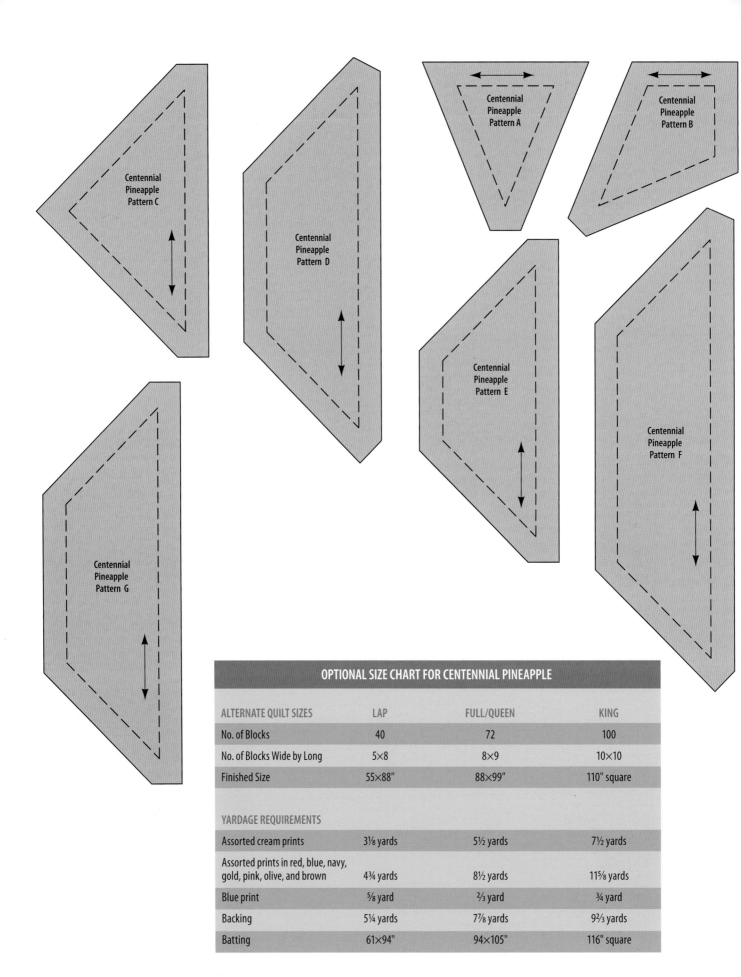

Centennial Pineapple Pattern C

Centennial Pineapple Pattern D

Centennial Pineapple Pattern A

Centennial Pineapple Pattern B

Centennial Pineapple Pattern E

Centennial Pineapple Pattern F

Centennial Pineapple Pattern G

OPTIONAL SIZE CHART FOR CENTENNIAL PINEAPPLE

ALTERNATE QUILT SIZES	LAP	FULL/QUEEN	KING
No. of Blocks	40	72	100
No. of Blocks Wide by Long	5×8	8×9	10×10
Finished Size	55×88"	88×99"	110" square
YARDAGE REQUIREMENTS			
Assorted cream prints	3⅛ yards	5½ yards	7½ yards
Assorted prints in red, blue, navy, gold, pink, olive, and brown	4¾ yards	8½ yards	11⅝ yards
Blue print	⅝ yard	⅔ yard	¾ yard
Backing	5¼ yards	7⅞ yards	9⅔ yards
Batting	61×94"	94×105"	116" square

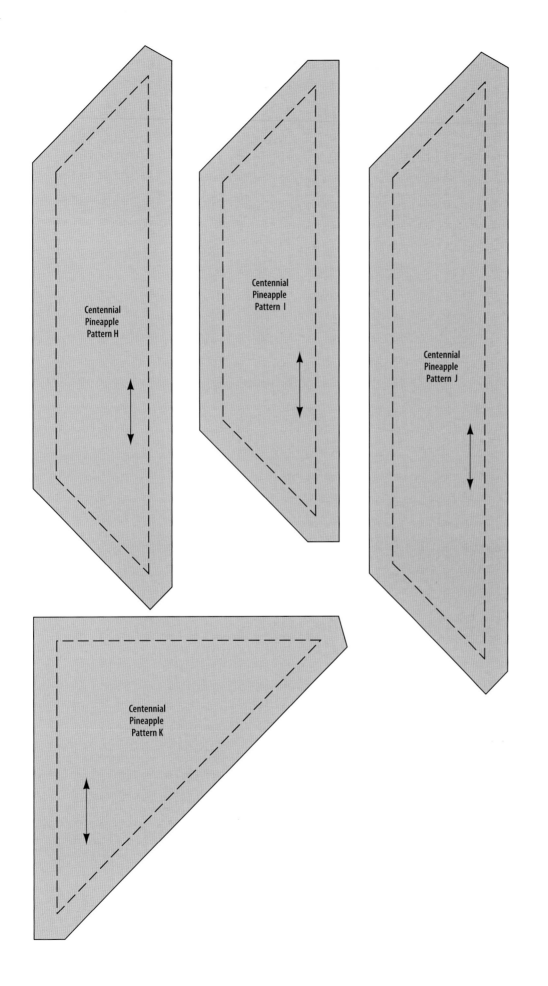

Centennial
Pineapple
Pattern H

Centennial
Pineapple
Pattern I

Centennial
Pineapple
Pattern J

Centennial
Pineapple
Pattern K

country charm

Designed by Kim Diehl Photographed by Greg Scheidemann

Designer Kim Diehl used a touch of floral appliqué with button embellishments to accent tiny patchwork X blocks on her small quilt.

materials

½ yard total of assorted medium and dark print scraps for blocks, appliqués, and binding
¼ yard total of assorted light prints for blocks
18×22" piece (fat quarter) of red stripe for border
9×22" piece (fat eighth) of black print for border
⅛ yard total of assorted green prints for appliqué stems

⅝ yard of backing fabric
21×24" of quilt batting
22 assorted buttons ranging from ⁷⁄₁₆" to ⅝" in diameter
Freezer paper (optional)
Fabric basting glue or glue stick (optional)
Monofilament thread: .004 (optional)

Finished quilt top: 15×18"
Finished block: 3" square

Quantities specified for 44/45"-wide, 100% cotton fabrics. All measurements include a ¼" seam allowance. Sew with right sides together unless otherwise stated.

cut the fabrics

To make the best use of your fabrics, cut the pieces in the order that follows.

from assorted medium and dark print scraps, cut:
- Enough 2½"-wide strips to total 72" in length for binding
- 160—1¼" square

from assorted light prints, cut:
- 48—2" squares

from red stripe, cut:
- 2—3½×12½" border strips
- 2—3½×9½" border strips

from black print, cut:
- 4—3½" squares

from assorted green prints, cut:
- 2—1¼×9" strips
- 2—1¼×7½" strips

piece the X blocks

1. Use a quilter's pencil to mark a diagonal line on the wrong side of 144 of the assorted medium and dark print 1¼" squares.

2. Align two marked print 1¼" squares with opposite corners of a light print 2" square (see Diagram 1). Sew on the drawn lines; trim away the excess fabric, leaving ¼" seam allowances. Press the attached triangles open.

Diagram 1

3. Align a marked print square with one corner of the Step 2 unit (see Diagram 2). Sew on the drawn line; trim away the excess fabric, leaving a ¼" seam allowance. Press the attached triangle open to make a pieced block unit.

Diagram 2

4. Repeat steps 2 and 3 to make a total of 48 pieced block units.

5. Referring to Diagram 3, lay out four pieced block units in pairs. Sew together the pairs; press the seam allowances in opposite directions. Then join the pairs to make an X

Diagram 3

block. Press the seam allowance in one direction. The pieced X block should measure 3½" square, including the seam allowances. Repeat to make a total of 12 X blocks.

assemble the quilt top

1. Referring to the Quilt Assembly Diagram, lay out the 12 X blocks in four horizontal rows. Sew together the blocks in each row. Press the seam allowances in one direction, alternating the direction with each row. Then join the

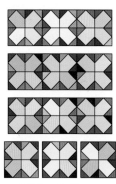

Quilt Assembly Diagram

rows to make the quilt center. Press the seam allowances in one direction. The pieced quilt center should measure 9½×12½", including the seam allowances.

2. Sew a red stripe 3½×12½" border strip to each long edge of the pieced quilt center. Press the seam allowances toward the red stripe border.

3. Sew a black print 3½" square to each end of the red stripe 3½×9½" border strips. Press the seam allowances toward the black print squares. The pieced border strips should measure 3½×15½", including seam allowances. Join a pieced border strip to each remaining edge of the pieced quilt center to complete the quilt top. Press the seam allowances toward the red stripe border.

prepare the appliqués

Kim uses a freezer-paper method for appliquéing. The instructions that follow are for this technique. If you prefer, choose your favorite method of appliqué. The patterns are on *page 44.*

1. Referring to Diagram 4, sew together four assorted medium and dark print 1¼" squares in pairs. Press the seam allowances in opposite directions. Join the pairs to make a Four-Patch unit. Press the seam allowance in one direction. The pieced Four-Patch unit should measure 2" square, including the seam allowances. Repeat to make a total of four Four-Patch units.

Diagram 4

2. Position the freezer paper, shiny side down, over the patterns. With a pencil, trace each pattern the number of times indicated. Cut out the freezer-paper shapes on the traced lines.

3. Place a small amount of fabric glue on the matte side of the freezer-paper shapes and anchor them to the backs of the designated fabrics, leaving approximately ½" between shapes for seam allowances.

4. Cut out the fabric shapes about ¼" beyond the freezer-paper edges to make the appliqués. Clip curves as necessary.

from assorted medium and dark scraps, cut:
- 4 *each* of patterns A and C
- 10 of Pattern B
- 8 of Pattern B reversed

from the pieced four-patch units, cut:
- 4 of Pattern D (centering the pattern atop the intersection of the four squares)

5. Use the point of a hot iron on a dry setting to press the seam allowances under and onto the shiny side of the freezer-paper shapes.

6. Fold a green print 1¼×9" strip in half lengthwise with the wrong side inside; press. Stitching a scant ¼" from the edges, sew together the long edges (see Diagram 5). Trim the seam allowance to ⅛". Refold the strip, centering the seam in the back to make a long stem appliqué; press.

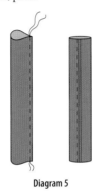

Diagram 5

7. Repeat Step 6 with the remaining assorted green print 1¼-wide strips to make a total of two long stem appliqués and two short stem appliqués.

appliqué the quilt top

1. Referring to the Appliqué Placement Diagram *above right,* position the appliqué pieces on the quilt top; baste in place. Working from the bottom layer to the top, use monofilament thread to machine-blindstitch or zigzag-stitch the pieces in place. ***Note:*** If you are appliquéing by hand, leave a ½" opening for removing the freezer-paper shapes; if you are appliquéing by machine, this opening is not needed (see Step 2 below).

Appliqué Placement Diagram

2. Once all the pieces are appliquéd in place, on the back side of each appliqué, trim away the excess quilt top fabric, leaving a ¼" seam allowance. With your fingertip or the tip of your needle, gently peel the freezer paper away from the fabric.

complete the quilt

1. Layer the appliquéd quilt top, batting, and backing according to the instructions in Quilting Basics, which begins on *page 45.*

2. Quilt as desired. Kim Diehl hand-quilted intersecting diagonal lines over the block centers. She stitched in the ditch between blocks and channel-quilted the borders using the stripes as a guide. She outline-quilted each appliqué to emphasize its shape.

3. Piece the assorted medium and dark print 2½"-wide strips to make a 72"-long binding strip.

4. Use the 72"-long strip to bind the quilt according to the instructions in Quilting Basics.

5. Sew a button to each flower center and at each X marked on the Appliqué Placement Diagram.

OPTIONAL SIZE CHART FOR COUNTRY CHARM			
ALTERNATE QUILT SIZES	WALL	TWIN	FULL
No. of Blocks	16	35	56
No. of Blocks Wide by Long	4×4	5×7	7×8
Finished Size	49" square	60×82"	82×93"
YARDAGE REQUIREMENTS			
No. of assorted yellow print 18×22" pieces	8	14	20
Dark blue print	1¼ yards	1¾ yards	2⅜ yards
No. of assorted blue print 18×22" pieces	12	20	29
Backing	3⅛ yards	5 yards	7⅓ yards
Batting	55" square	66×88"	88×99"

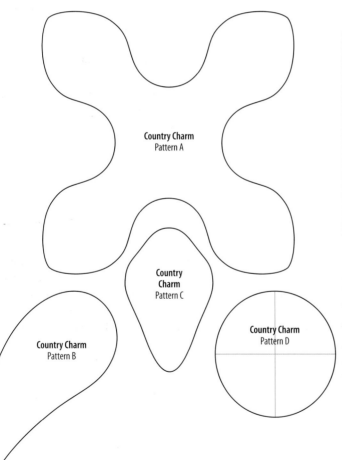

Country Charm
Pattern A

Country Charm
Pattern C

Country Charm
Pattern B

Country Charm
Pattern D

color option

This lighter, brighter version of Country Charm utilizes tone-on-tone fabrics and textured solids. Using fabrics with subtle variations reveals surprising details, especially when the quilt is viewed up close—which is often the case with a small quilt. In this case, the fabric used in the border looks like denim chambray.

quilting basics

Refer to this handy guide to cut, piece, assemble, and finish your quilt with ease.

tools

Cutting

Acrylic ruler: To aid in making perfectly straight cuts with a rotary cutter, choose a ruler of thick, clear plastic. Many sizes are available. A 6×24" ruler marked in ¼" increments with 30°, 45°, and 60° angles is a good first purchase.

Rotary-cutting mat: A rotary cutter should always be used with a mat designed specifically for it. In addition to protecting the table, the mat helps keep the fabric from shifting while you cut. Often these mats are described as self-healing, meaning the blade does not leave slash marks or grooves in the surface, even after repeated usage. While many shapes and styles are available, a 16×23" mat marked with a 1" grid, with hash marks at ⅛" increments and 45° and 60° angles is a good choice.

Rotary cutter: The round blade of a rotary cutter will cut up to six layers of fabric at once. Because the blade is so sharp, be sure to purchase one with a safety guard and keep the guard over the blade when you're not cutting. The blade can be removed from the handle and replaced when it gets dull. Commonly available in three sizes, a good first blade is a 45 mm.

Scissors: You'll need one pair for cutting fabric and another for cutting paper and plastic.

Pencils and other marking tools: Marks made with special quilt markers are easy to remove after sewing.

Template plastic: This slightly frosted plastic comes in sheets about ¹⁄₁₆" thick.

Piecing

Iron and ironing board

Sewing thread: Use 100% cotton thread.

Sewing machine: Any machine in good working order with well-adjusted tension will produce pucker-free patchwork seams.

choose your fabrics

Most patterns, including those in this book, specify quantities for 44/45"-wide fabrics unless otherwise noted. Our projects call for a little extra yardage in length to allow for minor errors and slight shrinkage.

prepare your fabrics

We recommend you prewash a scrap of each fabric to test it for shrinkage and bleeding. If you choose to prewash an entire fabric piece, unfold it to a single layer. Wash it in warm water, which will allow the fabric to shrink and/or bleed. If the fabric bleeds, rinse it until the water runs clear. Do not use it in a quilt if it hasn't stopped bleeding. Hang the fabric to dry, or tumble it in the dryer until slightly damp; press well.

select the batting

For a small beginner project, a thin cotton batting is a good choice. It has a tendency to "stick" to fabric so it requires less basting. Also, it's easy to stitch. It's wise to follow the stitch density (distance between rows of stitching required to keep the batting from shifting and wadding up inside the quilt) recommendation printed on the packaging.

Polyester batting is lightweight and readily available. In general, it springs back to its original height when compressed, adding a puffiness to quilts. It tends to "beard" (work out between the weave of the fabric) more than natural fibers. Polyester fleece is denser and works well for pillow tops and place mats.

Wool batting has good loft retention and absorbs moisture, making it ideal for cool, damp climates. Read the label carefully before purchasing a wool batting because it may require special handling.

cutting bias strips

Strips for curved appliqué pattern pieces and for binding curved edges should be cut on the bias (diagonally across the grain of a woven fabric), which runs at a 45° angle to the selvage and has the most stretch.

To cut bias strips, begin with a fabric square or rectangle; use an acrylic ruler to square up the left edge. Make a cut at a 45° angle to the left edge (see Bias Strip Diagram *below*). Handle the diagonal edges carefully to avoid distorting the bias. To cut a strip, measure the desired width from the 45° cut edge; cut parallel to the edge. Cut enough strips to total the length needed.

Bias Strip Diagram

make templates

A template is a pattern made from sturdy material so you can trace around it many times without wearing away the edges. Acrylic templates for many common shapes are available at quilt shops. Or, you can make your own by duplicating printed patterns on plastic.

To make permanent templates, try using easy-to-cut template plastic, available at crafts supply stores. This material lasts indefinitely, and its transparency allows you to trace the pattern directly onto its surface.

To make a template, lay the plastic over a printed pattern. Trace the pattern onto the plastic using a ruler and a permanent marker. This will ensure straight lines, accurate corners, and permanency.

For hand piecing and appliqué, make templates the exact size the finished pieces will be, without seam allowances, by tracing the patterns' dashed lines.

For machine piecing, make templates that include the seam allowances.

For easy reference, mark each template with its letter designation, grain line if noted, and block name. Verify the template's size by placing it over the printed pattern. Templates must be accurate or the error, however small, will compound many times as you assemble a quilt. To check the accuracy of your templates, make a test block before cutting the fabric pieces for an entire quilt.

trace templates

To mark on fabric, use a pencil, white dressmaker's pencil, chalk, or a special fabric marker that makes a thin, accurate line. Do not use a ballpoint or ink pen; it may bleed if washed. Test all marking tools on a fabric scrap before using them.

To trace pieces that will be used for hand piecing or appliqué, place templates facedown on the wrong side of the fabric; position the templates at least ½" apart (see Diagram 1).

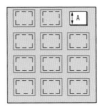

Diagram 1

The traced lines on the fabric are the sewing lines. Mark cutting lines ¼" away from the sewing lines, or estimate the distance by eye when cutting out the pieces. For hand piecing, add a ¼" seam allowance; for hand appliqué, add a ³⁄₁₆" seam allowance.

Templates used to make pieces for machine piecing have seam allowances included so you can use common lines for efficient cutting. Place a template facedown on the wrong side of the fabric and trace; repeat, but do not leave spaces between the tracings (see Diagram 2). Using a rotary cutter and ruler, cut precisely on the drawn lines.

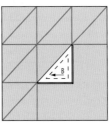

Diagram 2

plan for cutting

Our project instructions list pieces in the order they should be cut to make the best use of your fabrics. Always consider the fabric grain before cutting. The arrow on a pattern piece indicates which direction the fabric grain should run. One or more straight sides of the pattern piece should follow the fabric's lengthwise or crosswise grain.

The lengthwise grain, parallel to the selvage (the tightly finished edge), has the least amount of stretch. The crosswise grain, perpendicular to the selvage, has a little more give. The edge of any pattern piece that will be on the outside of a block or quilt should always be cut on the lengthwise grain. Do not use the selvage of a woven fabric in a quilt. When washed, it may shrink more than the rest of the fabric.

In projects larger than 42" in length or width, we specify that the border strips be cut the width (crosswise grain) of the fabric and pieced to use the least amount of fabric. If you'd prefer to cut the border strips on the lengthwise grain and not piece them, you'll need to refigure the yardage.

mitering borders

To add a border with mitered corners, first pin a border strip to a quilt top edge, matching the center of the strip and the center of the quilt top edge. Sew together, beginning and ending the seam ¼" from the quilt top corners (see Diagram 3). Allow excess border fabric to extend beyond the edges. Repeat with remaining border strips. Press the seam allowances toward the border strips.

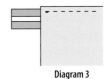

Diagram 3

At one corner, lap one border strip over the other (see Diagram 4). Align the edge of a 90° right triangle with the raw edge of the top strip so the long edge of the triangle intersects the border seam in the corner. With a pencil, draw along the edge of the triangle from the seam out to the raw edge. Place the bottom border strip on top and repeat the marking process.

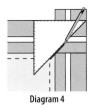

Diagram 4

With the right sides together, match the marked seam lines and pin (see Diagram 5).

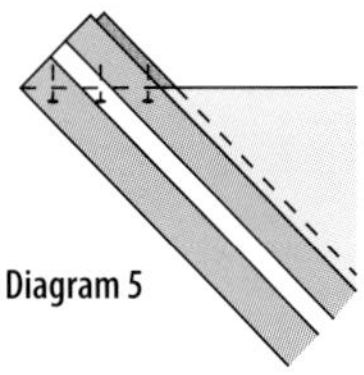

Diagram 5

Beginning with a backstitch at the inside corner, sew together the strips, stitching exactly on the marked lines. Check the right side to see that the corner lies flat. Trim the excess fabric, leaving a ¼" seam allowance. Press the seam open. Mark and sew the remaining corners in the same manner.

complete the quilt
Cut and piece the backing fabric to measure at least 3" bigger on all sides than the quilt top. Press all seam allowances open. With wrong sides together, layer the quilt top and backing fabric with the batting in between; baste. Quilt as desired.

The binding for most quilts is cut on the straight grain of the fabric. If your quilt has curved edges, cut the strips on the bias (see *page 45*). The cutting instructions for projects in this issue specify the number of binding strips or a total length needed to finish the quilt. The instructions also specify enough width for a French-fold, or double-layer, binding because it's easier to apply and adds durability.

Join the binding strips with diagonal seams (see Diagram 6) to make one continuous binding strip. Trim the excess fabric, leaving ¼" seam allowances. Press the seam allowances open. With the wrong side inside, fold under 1" at one end of the binding strip (see Diagram 7); press. Fold strip in half lengthwise (see Diagram 8).

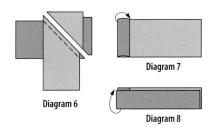

Diagram 7

Diagram 6

Diagram 8

Beginning in the center of one side, place the binding strip against the right side of the quilt top, aligning the binding strip's raw edges with the quilt top's raw edge (see Diagram 9). Sew through all layers, stopping ¼" from the corner (or a distance equal to the seam allowance you're using). Backstitch, then clip the threads. Remove the quilt from under the sewing-machine presser foot.

Fold the binding strip upward (see Diagram 10), creating a diagonal fold, and finger-press.

Holding the diagonal fold in place with your finger, bring the binding strip down in line with the next edge, making a horizontal fold that aligns with the quilt edge (see Diagram 11).

Start sewing again at the top of the horizontal fold, stitching through all layers. Sew around the quilt, turning each corner in the same manner.

When you return to the starting point, encase the binding strip's raw edge inside the folded end (see Diagram 12). Finish sewing to the starting point (see Diagram 13). Trim the batting and backing fabric even with the quilt top edges.

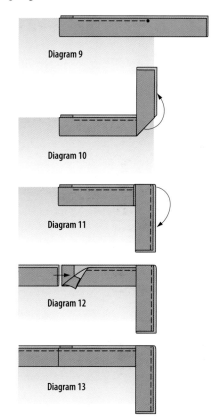

Diagram 9

Diagram 10

Diagram 11

Diagram 12

Diagram 13

Turn the binding over the edge to the back. Hand-stitch the binding to the backing fabric, making sure to cover any machine stitching.

To make mitered corners on the back, hand-stitch up to a corner; fold a miter in the binding. Take a stitch or two in the fold to secure it. Then stitch the binding in place up to the next corner. Finish each corner in the same manner.

Better Homes and Gardens®
Creative Collection™

Editorial Director John Riha

Editor in Chief Deborah Gore Ohrn

Executive Editor Karman Wittry Hotchkiss

Managing Editor Kathleen Armentrout

Contributing Editorial Manager Heidi Palkovic

Contributing Design Director Tracy DeVenney

Contributing Designer	Wendy Musgrave
Copy Chief	Mary Heaton
Contributing Copy Editor	Mary Helen Schiltz
Proofreader	Joleen F. Ross
Administrative Assistant	Lori Eggers

Publishing Group President
Jack Griffin

CORPORATION

President and CEO Stephen M. Lacy

Chairman of the Board William T. Kerr

In Memoriam
E. T. Meredith III (1933–2003)
